HTML

QuickStart Guide- Creating an Effective Website

Free Bonus!!!

We would like to offer you our FREE Guide to jump start you on a path to improve your life & Exclusive access to our Breakthrough Book Club!!! It's a place where we offer a NEW FREE E-book every week! Also our members are actively discussing, reviewing, and sharing their thoughts on the Book of The Week and on topics to help each other Breakthrough Life's Obstacles! With a Chance to win a $25 Gift Card EVERY Month! Please Enjoy Your FREE Guide & Access to the Breakthrough Book Club

https://publishfs.leadpages.co/the-breakthrough-book-club-d/

Table of Contents

Introduction

HTML or Hyper Text Markup Language is the most commonly used language for developing web pages. It was created in the year 1991 Berners-Lee. The standard HTML specification, HTML 2.0, was published in the year 1995. Another major version of this language, HTML 4.01 was released in late 1999. This was the most widely used version of HTML and it is now replaced by HTML 5, released in the year 2012. This is basically an extension to its previous version HTML 4.01.

This is for?

This tutorial on HTML is designed specifically for aspiring developers and web designers. This tutorial is explained in enough detail with practical examples and a simple overview so that it can be easily understood by beginners and provides enough knowledge to design their own webpages. You can get a higher level of expertise with some practice.

Prerequisites

The prerequisites for starting this tutorial are that it should have some basic knowledge of working with Linux operating system or Windows. In addition, you should also be familiar with:

- Using a text editor like editplus, notepad, notepad++ or any other text editor.

- Creating files and directories on your computer.

- Navigation within different directories.

- Different image formats like PNG, JPG, etc.

- Typing content into a file and saving them.

Chapter 1
Basic Tags in HTML

Heading Tags

Heading is the first thing in a document and every document starts with one. In HTML, you can set your heading in different sizes. There are six sizes of headings and they can be set using the elements **<h1>, <h2>, <h3>, <h4>, <h5>, and <h6>**. The browser will add a line before and after the heading while displaying. Here is an example.

Example

<!DOCTYPE html> <html> <head> <title>Example for Heading</title> </head> <body> <h1>This will be heading 1</h1> <h2>This will be heading 2</h2> <h3>This will be heading 3</h3> <h4>This will be heading

4</h4> <h5>This will be heading 5</h5> <h6>This will be heading 6</h6> </body> </html>

This code will produce the following output:

This will be heading 1

This will be heading 2

This will be heading 3

This will be heading 4

This will be heading 5

This will be Heading 6

Paragraph Tag

You can structure your content into paragraphs using the **<p>** tag. For making your text into a paragraph, you should place it in between the opening tag **<p>** and closing tag **</p>**. Here is an example.

Example

<!DOCTYPE html> <html> <head> <title>Example for Paragraph</title> </head> <body> <p>This text will be the first paragraph.</p> <p>This text will be the second

paragraph.</p> <p>This text will be the third paragraph.</p> </body> </html>

This code will produce the following output:

This text will be the first paragraph.

This text will be the second paragraph.

This text will be the third paragraph.

Line Break Tag

If you wish to add a line break in between your text, you can use the **
** element and any text following it will start in a new line. Some tags do not need closing tags and such tags are called empty elements. The **
** element is one such empty element. They are called so because no content goes in between them.

There is a space between **br** and / characters and if it is not added, older browsers will fail to render the line break. If the / is not added and just use **
**, it won't work in XHTML, as it is invalid. Here is an example.

Example

<!DOCTYPE html> <html> <head> <title>Example for Line Break</title> </head> <body> <p>Hey
 How are you doing today?.
 Good Luck
 Peter</p> </body> </html>

This code will produce the following output:

Hey

How are you doing today?

Good Luck

Peter

Centering Content

Sometimes you'll need to place your content at the center of
the table cell or page. For such cases, you can use the tag
<**center**>. Here is an example.

Example

<!DOCTYPE html> <html> <head> <title>Example for
Centering the Content</title> </head> <body> <p>This
text has the default alignment.</p> <center> <p>This
text is centered.</p> </center> </body> </html>

This code will produce the following the output:

This text has the default alignment.

This text is centered.

Horizontal Lines

You can visually break up the sections present in a document using the Horizontal lines. The **<hr>** tag is used for creating a horizontal line from the left margin to the right margin. This will break the line accordingly. For instance, if you want to insert a line break in between two paragraphs, you can use the code given below.

Example

```
<!DOCTYPE html> <html> <head> <title>Example for Horizontal Line</title> </head> <body> <p>This is the first paragraph. This is on the top of the line break.</p> <hr /> <p>This is the second paragraph. This is at the bottom of the line break. </p> </body> </html>
```

The above code will produce the following output:

This is the first paragraph. This is on the top of the line break.

This is the second paragraph. This is at the bottom of the line break.

The **<hr />** tag is also categorized as an **empty** element. This doesn't need opening tags and closing tags as there is no content going in between.

There is a space in between the characters **hr** and / in the **<hr />** element. If the space is omitted, older versions of browsers will have problem with the rendering the horizontal line and if the / is missed, it won't be a valid element in XHTML.

Preserve Formatting

In some cases your text should follow the same format as it is entered in the HTML document. You can make use of the <pre> tag in such cases. It means preformatted text.

Any text entered into between the tags <pre> and </pre> will have the same text format as seen in the source document. Here is an example.

Example

```
<!DOCTYPE html> <html> <head> <title>Example for Preserve Formatting</title> </head> <body> <pre> int main(void) {  printf("Hello World!\n");  // return 0;

} </pre> </body> </html>
```

The above code will produce the following output.

```
int main(void) {  printf("Hello World!\n");  // return 0;

}
```

Nonbreaking Spaces

In some cases you do not want your browser to split the words across lines. In such cases you can use the nonbreaking space entity ** ** instead of using the normal space. Have a look at the following example for a better understanding.

Example

Let us use the words James Bond 007 for our example and we do not want the browser to split these words. We will add to the nonbreaking space entity ** ** instead of space.

<!DOCTYPE html> <html> <head> <title>Example for Nonbreaking Spaces</title> </head> <body> <p>

The agent in the movie is "James Bond 007."</p> </body> </html>

Chapter 2

HTML Elements

An element in his family will be defined by starting tag. If other content can be contained within the element, it will have a closing tag. For the closing tag, the name of the element will be preceded with a /. Some of such elements are given below.

Start Tag	Content	End Tag
<i>	This is italic font content	</i>
<marquee>	This is marquee text content.	</marquee>
<p>	This is paragraph content.	</p>

Here, <i> and </i> is an element, <marquee> and </marquee> is another element. There are a few HTML elements that doesn't need closing tags, such as <br />, <hr />, <img />, etc. The HTML elements which doesn't require closing tags are called as **void elements**.

The HTML document has a tree for these elements and this tree specifies on how the documents of HTML should be built. It also specifies the type of content that is to be placed in what part of the document.

HTML Tag vs. Element

An element of HTML will be defined using a starting tag. If other content is placed inside it, it will have a closing tag.

For instance, <i> is the starting tag for italic text and </i> is the closing tag for it. But, <i>This text is italic</i> is a italic text element.

Nested Elements in HTML

HTML allows you to nest HTML elements within other HTML elements. Here is an example:

Example

<!DOCTYPE html> <html> <head> <title>Example for Nested Elements</title> </head> <body> <h2>This is <b>bold</b> heading</h2> <p>This is <i>italic</i> text</p> </body> </html>

The above code will produce the following output

This is **bold** heading

This is *italic* text

Attributes

Till now, we have seen some of the tags like paragraph tag <p>, heading tags <h1>, <h2> and a few other tags in the most simple form. These bags can be given some extra information known as attributes.

The characteristics of an element in HTML can be defined using an attribute. This will be placed inside the opening tag of the element and they contain two parts, **name** and **value.**

The **name** of the attribute is nothing but the property that you wish to set. For example, the font element carries attributes like color, size, type, etc., which are used for indicating the font color, font size and font type that is to be displayed on the page.

The **value** of the attribute is nothing but the value for the property that you wish to set. The value of an attribute should always be placed inside quotations. The examples below will show you the values that can be given to the above given **name**: Red, 3 and Georgia, as font color, size and type.

You should be careful when using names and values for attributes, as they are case sensitive. However, the W3C (World Wide Web Consortium), recommends the use of lowercase attributes and attribute values in their recommendation for HTML 4.

Here is an example.

Example

```
<!DOCTYPE html> <html> <head> <title>Align
Attribute Example</title> </head> <body> <p
align="right">This content will be aligned to the
right</p> <p align="center">This content will be aligned
to the center</p> <p align="left">This content will be
aligned to the left</p> </body> </html>
```

The above code will give us the following output:

This content will be aligned to the right.

This content will be aligned to the center.

This content will be aligned to the left.

Internationalization Attributes

In HTML, there are a total of three internationalization attributes. These are available for most of the XHTML elements, but not for all.

dir

lang

xml:lang

The dir Attribute

You can specify the text flow direction to the browser by using the **dir** attribute. This attribute can take two values, as shown in the table given below.

Value	Meaning
ltr	Left to right (this will be the default value)
rtl	Right to left (for languages such as Hebrew or Arabic that are read right to left)

Example

```
<!DOCTYPE html> <html
dir="rtl"> <head> <title>Display
Directions</title> </head> <body> This is how IE 5
renders right-to-left directed text. </body> </html>
```

The above code will produce the following output:

This is how IE 5 renders right-to-left directed text.

If the **dir** attribute is placed inside the<html> tag, it will determine how the text of the entire document will be presented. If this attitude is use the inside another tag, it will just to control the direction of the text contained in that specific tag.

The lang Attribute

You can indicate the main language that is to be used in your document by using the **lang** attribute. The only reason for keeping this attribute is HTML is for the backwards compatibility with previous versions of HTML. In the new XHTML documents, this attribute is replaced with the **xml:lang** attribute.

The *lang* attributes have the values as ISO 639 standard 2-character language codes. You can check the complete list of language codes with the **HTML Language Codes: ISO 639**.

Example

<!DOCTYPE html> <html lang="en"> <head> <title>English Language Page</title> </head> <body> This page is using English Language </body> </html>

The xml:lang Attribute

In XHTML, the *xml:lang* attribute is used as a replacement for the original *lang* attribute used in earlier versions of HTML. As mentioned above, the *xml:lang* attribute value should be an ISO-639 country code.

Generic Attributes

There are a few other attributes that can be readily used with most of the HTML tags. The list of those attributes is given in the table below.

Attribute	Options	Function
align	right, left, center	Horizontally aligns tags
valign	top, middle, bottom	Vertically aligns tags within an HTML element.
bgcolor	numeric, hexadecimal, RGB values	Places a background color behind an element
background	URL	Places a background image behind an element
id	User Defined	Names an element for use with Cascading Style Sheets.
class	User Defined	Classifies an element for use with Cascading Style Sheets.
width	Numeric Value	Specifies the width of tables, images, or table cells.
height	Numeric Value	Specifies the height of tables, images, or table cells.
title	User Defined	"Pop-up" title of the elements.

Chapter 3

Formatting in HTML

If you are familiar with using the word processor, you probably must also be similar with making text bold, italicized or underlined. There are a total of 10 options available in HTML and XHTML, which will indicate your text will appear.

Bold Text

Any content that is placed in between **<b>...</b>** element will be displayed as bold text. Here is an example.

Example

<!DOCTYPE html> <html> <head> <title>Example for Bold Text</title> </head> <body> <p>The following word will be in a <b>bold</b> typeface.</p> </body> </html>

The above code will produce the following output:

The following word will be in a **bold** typeface.

Italic Text

Any content that is placed in between **<i>...</i>** element will be displayed as italicized text. Here is an example.

Example

```
<!DOCTYPE html> <html> <head> <title>Example for Italic Text</title> </head> <body> <p>The following word will be in a <i>italicized</i> typeface.</p> </body> </html>
```

The above code will produce the following output:

The following word will be in an *italicized* typeface.

Underlined Text

Any content that is placed in between **<u>...</u>** element will be displayed as underlined text. Here is an example.

Example

```
<!DOCTYPE html> <html> <head> <title>Example for Underlined Text</title> </head> <body> <p>The following word will be in an <u>underlined</u> typeface.</p> </body> </html>
```

The above code will produce the following output:

The following word will be in an <u>underlined</u> typeface.

Strike Text

Any content that is placed in between **<strike>...</strike>** element will be displayed as struck text, is a thin line through the text. Here is an example.

Example

<!DOCTYPE html> <html> <head> <title>Strike Text Example</title> </head> <body> <p>The following word uses a <strike>strikethrough</strike> typeface.</p> </body> </html>

The above code will produce the following output:

The following word uses a ~~strikethrough~~ typeface.

Monospaced Font

Any content placed in between the **<tt>...</tt>** element will be displayed as monospaced font. Most of the available fonts are variable width fonts. This is because different letters have different widths. For instance the letter **w** is wider than **i.** With a monospaced font, every letter will have the same width. Here is an example.

Example

<!DOCTYPE html> <html> <head> <title>Example for Monospaced Font</title> </head> <body> <p>The following word uses a <tt>monospaced</tt> typeface.</p> </body> </html>

The above code will produce the following output:

The following word uses a monospaced typeface.

Superscript Text

You can use the **^{...}** element for adding a superscript on your web page. A superscript is nothing but the text with the same font with the same font size as the text surrounding it, but it will be displayed half a character's height above the surrounding text. Here is an example.

Example

<!DOCTYPE html> <html> <head> <title>Example for Superscript Text</title> </head> <body> <p>The following word uses a ^{superscript} typeface.</p> </body> </html>

The above code will produce the following output:

The following word uses a superscript typeface.

Subscript Text

You can use the **<sub>...</sub>** element for adding a subscript on your web page. A subscript is nothing but the text with the same font with the same font size as the text surrounding it, but it will be displayed half a character's height below the surrounding text. Here is an example.

Example

<!DOCTYPE html> <html> <head> <title>Example for Subscript Text</title> </head> <body> <p>The following word uses a <sub>subscript</sub> typeface.</p> </body> </html>

The above code will produce the following output:

The following word uses a $_{subscript}$ typeface.

Inserted Text

Any text that is placed in between the **<ins>...</ins>** element will be shown as inserted text. Here is an example.

Example

<!DOCTYPE html> <html> <head> <title>Example for Inserted Text</title> </head> <body> <p>I want to drink <del>cola</del> <ins>wine</ins></p> </body> </html>

The above code will produce the following output:

I want to drink cola wine

Deleted Text

Any text that is placed in between the **<del>...</del>** element will be shown as deleted text. Here is an example.

Example

<!DOCTYPE html> <html> <head> <title>Example for Deleted Text</title> </head> <body> <p>I want to drink <del>cola</del> <ins>wine</ins></p> </body> </html>

The above code will produce the following output:

I want to drink wine

Larger Text

Any content placed inside the element **<big>...</big>** will be displayed as a one size larger font than the rest of the content surrounding it. Here is an example explaining larger text.

Example

<!DOCTYPE html> <html> <head> <title>Example for Larger Text</title> </head> <body> <p>You can

add<big>larger</big> text in middle of a sentence using this.</p> </body> </html>

This above code will produce the following output:

You can add larger text in middle of a sentence using this.

Smaller Text

Any content placed inside the element **<small>...</small>** will be displayed as a one size smaller font than the rest of the content surrounding it. Here is an example explaining smaller text.

Example

<!DOCTYPE html> <html> <head> <title>Example for Smaller Text</title> </head> <body> <p> You can add <small>smaller</small> text in middle of a sentence using this.</p> </body> </html>

This above code will produce the following output:

You can add smaller text in middle of a sentence using this.

Grouping Content

You can use the elements **<div>** and **<span>** for grouping several elements together for creating sections or subsections in a page. Here is an example.

Example

```
<!DOCTYPE html> <html> <head> <title>Example for
Div Tag</title> </head> <body> <div id="menu"
align="middle" > <a href="/index.htm">HOME</a> | <a
href="/about/contact_us.htm">CONTACT</a> | <a
href="/about/index.htm">ABOUT</a> </div> <div
id="content" align="left" bgcolor="white"> <h4>Some
Content</h4> <p>The content will go
here.....</p> </div> </body> </html>
```

This will produce the following output:

HOME | CONTACT | ABOUT

SOME CONTENT

The content will go here.....

On the other hand, the <span> element can only be used for grouping inline elements. In cases where you need to group a part of a paragraph or a sentence together, you can make use of the <span> element. Here is an example.

Example

```
<!DOCTYPE html> <html> <head> <title>Example for
Span Tag</title> </head> <body> <p>This is the
```

example of span tag and the div tag along with CSS</p> </body> </html>

The above code will produce the following output.

This is the example of span tag and the div tag along with CSS

The above tags are used alongside CSS, which allow you to attach a style to a particular section of a page.

Chapter 4
HTML Phrase Tags

The phrase tags in HTML are designed for performing specific purposes. They look similar to other tags like <b>, <i>, <pre>, and <tt>, which we have already seen in our previous chapters. In this chapter we will go through the important phrase tags in HTML.

Emphasized Text

Any content that is placed in between the **...** element will be shown as emphasized text. Here is an example.

Example:

<!DOCTYPE html> <html> <head> <title>Example for Emphasized   Text</title> </head> <body> <p>The

following word uses a <em>emphasized</em> typeface.</p> </body> </html>

The above code will produce the following output:

The following word uses an *emphasized* typeface.

Marked Text

Any content that is placed in between the **<mark>...</mark>** element will be shown as marked text, with a yellow link. Here is an example.

Example

<!DOCTYPE html> <html> <head> <title>Marked Text Example</title> </head> <body> <p>The following word has been <mark>marked</mark> with yellow</p> </body> </html>

The above code will produce the following output:

The following word has been marked with yellow.

Strong Text

Any content that is placed in between the **<strong>...</strong>** element will be shown as important text. Here is an example.

Example

```
<!DOCTYPE html> <html> <head> <title>Strong Text
Example</title> </head> <body> <p>The following
word uses a <strong>strong</strong>
typeface.</p> </body> </html>
```

The above code will produce the following output:

The following word uses a **strong** typeface.

Text Abbreviation

In HTML, you are allowed to abbreviate your text. You can do it by placing the text inside the opening **<abbr>** and closing**</abbr>** tags. The full description should be added in the title attribute and nothing else, if present. Here is an example.

Example

```
<!DOCTYPE html> <html> <head> <title>Text
Abbreviation</title> </head> <body> <p>My best
friend's name is <abbr
title="Abigail">Abi</abbr>.</p> </body> </html>
```

The above code will produce the following output:

My best friend's name is Abi.

Acronym Element

You can indicate your text as an acronym in HTML by using the**<acronym>** element. You should place your text in between the opening tag <acronym> and closing tag </acronym> for indicating it as an acronym. Here is an example.

Example

```
<!DOCTYPE html> <html> <head> <title>Acronym Example</title> </head> <body> <p>This chapter covers marking up text in <acronym>XHTML</acronym>.</p> </body> </html>
```

The above code will produce the following output:

This chapter covers marking up text in XHTML.

Text Direction

The element **<bdo>...</bdo>** stands for Bi-Directional Override. You can override the text direction using this element. Here is an example.

Example

```
<!DOCTYPE html> <html> <head> <title>Example for Text Direction</title> </head> <body> <p>This text
```

goes from left to right.</p> <p><bdo dir="rtl">This text goes from right to left.</bdo></p> </body> </html>

The above code will produce the following output:

This text goes from left to right.

This text goes from right to left.

Special Terms

You can introduce special terms on your web page on for doing it; you can use the element **<dfn>...</dfn>**. This is very much similar to italicized text in the middle of a paragraph.

You would typically use the element <dfn> when you introduce a key term for the first time. The recent browsers will render the text of the <dfn> element in and italicized format. Here is an example.

Example

<!DOCTYPE html> <html> <head> <title>Special Terms Example</title> </head> <body> <p>The following word is a <dfn>special</dfn> term.</p> </body> </html>

The above code will produce the following output:

The following word is a special term.

Quoting Text

In HTML, you can quote a passage from a different source. For doing it, you should place the content in between the opening tag **<blockquote>** and closing tag **</blockquote>**.

Any text placed inside this element will usually be intended from left and right edges of the text surrounding it. Sometimes it uses italicized font. Here is an example.

Example

<!DOCTYPE html> <html> <head> <title>Blockquote Example</title> </head> <body> <p>The following description of XHTML is taken from the W3C Web site:</p> <blockquote>XHTML 1.0 is the W3C's first Recommendation for XHTML, following on from earlier work on HTML 4.01, HTML 4.0, HTML 3.2 and HTML 2.0.</blockquote> </body> </html>

The above code will produce the following output:

The following description of XHTML is taken from the W3C Web site:

XHTML 1.0 is the W3C's first Recommendation for XHTML, following on from earlier work on HTML 4.01, HTML 4.0, HTML 3.2 and HTML 2.0.

Short Quotations

You can add double quotes inside a sentence by using the **<q>...</q>** element. Here is an example.

Example

```
<!DOCTYPE html> <html> <head> <title>Example for Double Quote</title> </head> <body> <p>Paul is in Spain, <q>I think I am right</q>.</p> </body> </html>
```

The above code will produce the following output:

Paul is in Spain, I think I am right.

Text Citations

When you are quoting some text, by placing the source between the opening and closing tags **<cite> </cite>**, you can indicate the source. Here is an example.

Example

```
<!DOCTYPE html> <html> <head> <title>Example for Citations</title> </head> <body> <p>This     HTML
```

tutorial is derived from <cite>W3 Standard for HTML</cite>.</p> </body> </html>

The above code will produce the following output:

This HTML tutorial is derived from W3 Standard for HTML.

Computer Code

If you are adding any programming code to your web page, you should place it inside the opening tag **<code>** and closing tag **</code>**. The content placed inside this element will usually be presented in the monospaced font, like any other called in other programming books. Here is an example.

Example

<!DOCTYPE html> <html> <head> <title>Example Computer Code</title> </head> <body> <p>This is regular text. <code>This is code.</code> This is regular text.</p> </body> </html>

The above code will produce the following output:

This is regular text. This is code. This is regular text.

Keyboard Text

In some situations, you will need your reader to type text using his keyboard. In such situations you can make use of the element **<kbd>...</kbd>**. This element will indicate a text that is to be typed. Here is an example.

Example

<!DOCTYPE html> <html> <head> <title>Example for Keyboard Text</title> </head> <body> <p>Regular text. <kbd>This is inside kbd element</kbd> Regular text.</p> </body> </html>

The above code will produce the following output:

Regular text. This is inside kbd element Regular text.

Programming Variables

Usually, this element will be used along with the elements **<code>** and **<pre>** for indicating that the content placed inside this element is variable. Here is an example.

Example

<!DOCTYPE html> <html> <head> <title>Example Variable
Text</title> </head> <body> <p><code>document.writ e("<var>user-id</var>")</code></p> </body> </html>

The above code will produce the following output:

document.write("user-id")

Program Output

The sample output of a program can be indicated using the element **<samp>...</samp>**. Script can also be indicated using this. However, it is usually used for documenting coding concepts or programming. Here is an example.

Example

<!DOCTYPE html> <html> <head> <title>Example Program Output</title> </head> <body> <p>The result of the program is <samp>Hello World!</samp></p> </body> </html>

The above code will produce the following output:

The result of the program is Hello World!

Address Text

You can give the address using the **<address>...</address>** element. Here is an example.

Example

<!DOCTYPE html> <html> <head> <title>Example for Address</title> </head> <body> <address>1719 c, David

Drive,   Marietta,   Atlanta,   Georgia
</address> </body> </html>

The above code will produce the following output:

1719 c, David Drive, Marietta, Atlanta, Georgia

Chapter 5
Meta Tags

In HTML, you are allowed to specifying metadata, which is the additional important information regarding the document, in different ways. You can use the META elements for including name/value pairs for describing the properties of the document, such as document author, author, expiry date, the list of keywords, etc.,

Such additional information can be provided using the **<meta>** tag. There are no closing tags for the Meta tag and hence it is an empty element. Though it is an empty element, but the information can be passed through its attributes.

In general, you can add more than one meta tags to your document, basing on the information that you are adding to your document. The physical appearance of your document will not have any effect because of meta tags. From the application point of view, it doesn't matter if meta tags are included or not.

Adding Meta Tags to Your Documents

You can provide a Meta data to your pages by adding <meta> tags within The document's header, represented by the tags **<head>** and **</head>**. In addition to their core attributes, they can have the following attributes:

Attribute	Description
Name	Name for the property. Can be anything. Examples include, keywords, description, author, revised, generator etc.
content	Specifies the property's value.
scheme	Specifies a scheme to interpret the property's value (as declared in the content attribute).
h t t p - equiv	Used for http response message headers. For example http-equiv can be used to refresh the page or to set a cookie. Values include content-type, expires, refresh and set-cookie.

Specifying Keywords

Important keywords that are related to the document can be specified using <meta> tag. These keywords will be later used by various search engines. They will also be used for indexing your page for search. Here is an example.

Example

In the below example, we will add the words Ducati, Aprilia and BMW as the important keywords related to the document.

```
<!DOCTYPE html> <html> <head> <title>Meta Tags
Example</title> <meta                name="keywords"
content="Ducati,          Aprilia,          BMW"
/> </head> <body> <p>Hello
World!</p> </body> </html>
```

The above code will produce the following output:

Hello World!

Document Description

You can provide a short description of your document by
using <meta> tags. Similar to keywords, the subscription
will also be used by search engines while indexing the web
page for searching purposes. Here is an example.

Example

```
<!DOCTYPE html> <html> <head> <title>Example for
Meta        Tags</title> <meta        name="keywords"
content="Ducati,     Aprilia,     BMW"        /> <meta
name="description" content="Learning about Meta Tags."
/> </head> <body> <p>Hello
World!</p> </body> </html>
```

Document Revision Date

The <meta> tag can be used for providing information regarding the last updation of the document. Various web browsers use this information while refreshing your web page. Here is an example.

Example

<!DOCTYPE html> <html> <head> <title>Meta Tags Example</title> <meta name="keywords" content="Ducati, Aprilia, BMW" /> <meta name="description" content="Learning about Meta Tags." /> <meta name="revised" content="Topgear, 7/7/15" /> </head> <body> <p>Hello HTML5!</p> </body> </html>

Document Refreshing

You can use the <meta> tag for specifying the duration on when to auto refresh your page. Here is an example.

Example

If you wish to make your web page refreshed automatically for every 10 seconds, use the below syntax.

Syntax:

```
<!DOCTYPE html> <html> <head> <title>Meta Tags
Example</title> <meta               name="keywords"
content="Ducati,      Aprilia,     BMW"      /> <meta
name="description" content="Learning about Meta Tags."
/> <meta   name="revised"   content="Topgear,   7/7/15"
/> <meta        http-equiv="refresh"        content="10"
/> </head> <body> <p>Hello
HTML5!</p> </body> </html>
```

Page Redirection

Using <meta> tag, you can redirect your web page to other web pages. You can actually specify the duration when you want to redirect the page by specifying the number of seconds. Here is an example.

Example

In the following example, the current page will be redirected to another page after 10 seconds. If you leave the content attribute unspecified, the current web page will be redirected immediately.

```
<!DOCTYPE html> <html> <head> <title>Meta Tags
Example</title> <meta               name="keywords"
content="Ducati,      Aprilia,     BMW"      /> <meta
```

name="description" content="Learning about Meta Tags."
/> <meta name="revised" content="Topgear, 7/7/15"
/> <meta http-equiv="refresh" content="5;
url=http://www.topgear.com"
/> </head> <body> <p>Hello
HTML5!</p> </body> </html>

Setting Cookies

Cookies are nothing but a data that is stored on your computer in the form of small text files. Cookies are exchanged between the web server and the web browser for keeping track on the information that the web application needs.

Using <meta> tag, the cookies can be stored on the client side and of this information can be later used by the web server for tracking the visitor of its site.

Example

In the following example, the current page will be redirected to another page after 10 seconds. If you leave the content attribute unspecified, the current web page will be redirected immediately.

<!DOCTYPE html> <html> <head> <title>Meta Tags
Example</title> <meta name="keywords"

content="Ducati,   Aprilia,   BMW"   /> <meta name="description" content="Learning about Meta Tags." /> <meta name="revised" content="Topgear, 7/Jul/15" /> <meta http-equiv="cookie" content="userid=xyz; expires=Wednesday,   08-Aug-15   23:59:59   GMT;" /> </head> <body> <p>Hello HTML5!</p> </body> </html>

If the expiration date and time are not included, the cookie will then be considered as a session cooking. Session cookies will be deleted when the browser is closed.

Setting Author Name

You can set an author name in a web page using meta tag. See an example below:

Example

<!DOCTYPE html> <html> <head> <title>Meta Tags Example</title> <meta   name="keywords" content="Ducati,   Aprilia,   BMW"   /> <meta name="description" content="Learning about Meta Tags." /> <meta name="author" content="Mahnaz Mohtashim" /> </head> <body> <p>Hello HTML5!</p> </body> </html>

Specify Character Set

You can use <meta> tag to specify character set used within the webpage.

Example

By default, Web servers and Web browsers use ISO-8859-1 (Latin1) encoding to process Web pages. Following is an example to set UTF-8 encoding:

```
<!DOCTYPE html> <html> <head> <title>Meta Tags Example</title> <meta name="keywords" content="Ducati, Aprilia, BMW" /> <meta name="description" content="Learning about Meta Tags." /> <meta name="author" content="Mahnaz Mohtashim" /> <meta http-equiv="Content-Type" content="text/html; charset=UTF-8" /> </head> <body> <p>Hello HTML5!</p> </body> </html>
```

To serve the static page with traditional Chinese characters, the webpage must contain a <meta> tag to set Big5 encoding:

```
<!DOCTYPE html> <html> <head> <title>Meta Tags Example</title> <meta name="keywords" content="Ducati, Aprilia, BMW" /> <meta
```

name="description" content="Learning about Meta Tags." /> <meta name="author" content="Mahnaz Mohtashim" /> <meta http-equiv="Content-Type" content="text/html; charset=Big5" /> </head> <body> <p>Hello HTML5!</p> </body> </html>

Chapter 6

Comments

Comments are nothing but pieces of code that are ignored by web browser. Adding comments to the HTML code is a very good practice, especially for complex documents. Comments indicate different sections of a document. They can also be used for indicating other notes to other persons looking at the code. By increasing the code readability, comments help users to understand code easily.

For adding a comment in HTML, you need to place the content in between the tags **<!-- ... -->**. Any content that is placed inside these tags will be considered as comments and the browser will completely ignore them. Here is an example

Example

```
<!DOCTYPE html> <html> <head> <!-- Document Header Starts --> <title>This is document title</title> </head> <!-- Document Header Ends --
```

> <body> <p>The content of the document goes here.....</p> </body> </html>

This code will produce the output which displays the content placed inside the paragraph tag but it will hide the content placed inside the comment tags.

The content of the document goes here.....

Valid vs. Invalid Comments

Comments cannot be nested; this means that you cannot place a comment inside another comment. You should always ensure that there are no spaces given at the start of the comment string. The '--' (double dash sequence) may not appear within a comments except in the closing tag (-->). Here is an example.

Example

In this example, we will give a valid comment and it will be ignored by the browser.

<!DOCTYPE html> <html> <head> <title>Example for Comment</title> </head> <body> <!-- This comment is valid --> <p>The content of the document goes here.....</p> </body> </html>

The above code will produce the following output:

The content of the document goes here.....

The following example will have an invalid comment. Browsers do not hide invalid comments and they display them as content. We will add an extra space in between the opening < and !.

```
<!DOCTYPE html> <html> <head>  <title>Example for Invalid Comment</title> </head>  <body> < !--  This comment is not a valid one --> <p>The content of the document goes here.....</p> </body> </html>
```

The above code will produce the following output:

< !-- This comment is not a valid one -->

The content of the document goes here.....

Multiline Comments

So far, we have only discussed about single line comments. However, HTML also supports the multi-line comments.

You can increase the code readability by adding comments in multiple lines by using a special beginning and ending tags <!-- and --> that are placed in front of the first line and after the last line as given in the example shown below.

Example

```
<!DOCTYPE html><html> <head>     <title>Multiline
Comments</title> </head>   <body> <!--   This is an
example of multiline comment and

it can be extended to any number of

lines you like.

--> <p>The    content    of    the    document    goes
here.....</p> </body> </html>
```

The above code will produce the following output:

The content of the document goes here.....

Conditional Comments

The conditional comments do not work on any other browser other than Internet Explorer. Other browsers ignore conditional comments. The support for conditional comments started from Internet Explorer 5. They can be used for giving conditional instructions for different Internet Explorer versions. Here is an example.

Example

```
<!DOCTYPE html><html> <head>     <title>Example for
Conditional  Comments</title>   <!--[if  IE  6]>  Special
```

instructions for IE 6 here <![endif]--> </head> <body> <p>The content of the document goes here.....</p> </body> </html>

Conditional comments can be helpful in situations where you will need to use different style sheets, depending on the version of IE.

Using Comment Tag

A part of the HTML code can be made as a comment and there are a few browsers supporting the <comment> tag. Here is an example.

Example

<!DOCTYPE html><html> <head> <title>Using Comment Tag</title> </head> <body> <p>This is <comment>not</comment> Internet Explorer.</p> </body> </html>

The above code will produce the following output if you're using IE:

This is Internet Explorer.

The above code will produce the following output if you're using a different browser other than IE:

This is not Internet Explorer.

Commenting Script Code

In cases where you are using VBScript or JavaScript with your HTML code, it is wise to place the script code inside proper comments. This will make sure that they can be used with older browsers. Here is an example.

Example

```
<!DOCTYPE html><html> <head> <title>Commenting
Script Code</title> <script> <!--
   document.write("Hakuna Matata!") //--
> </script> </head> <body> <p>Hakuna,
Matata!</p> </body> </html>
```

The above code will produce the following output:

Hakuna Matata!

Hakuna, Matata!

Commenting Style Sheets

In cases where you are using style sheets with your HTML code, it is wise to place the style sheet code inside proper comments. This will make sure that they can be used with older browsers. We will learn about style sheets in a different chapter. Here is an example.

Example

```
<!DOCTYPE html><html> <head> <title>Commenting
Style Sheets</title> <style> <!-- .example { border:1px
solid #4a7d49; } //--> </style> </head> <body> <div
class="example">Good,
Morning!</div> </body> </html>
```

The above code will produce the following output:

Good, Morning!

Chapter 7
HTML Forms

Most websites have at least one page that asks its visitors for feedback, or requests them to subscribe by giving their e-mail. To be able to do this, you need to have several text boxes in the page, where the users give their inputs. Forms are used pretty much everywhere, though it goes unnoticed. When you log into your e-mail, Facebook, or anything that requires a username and password, you're using a form to input your data. This can be done in HTML by using forms, and its elements.

The idea behind a form is that the visitor uses the text box to input some data, and the data gets posted to a back-end application like ASP or PHP script. This application can be configured to perform whatever action the webpage creator wants using his own logical algorithms. Listed below are some commonly used elements and attribute which you *must* know about to create a form that can capture your visitor's attention:

Input

The most important element out there, you use this to get the input from the user. There are various input attributes like text, radio buttons, and the submit button. Radio buttons are used to select from different options which you give, and the other two are fairly straightforward to understand. The syntax is <input>.

TextArea

When you want your user to enter something that goes beyond a single line, such as a paragraph to describe their professional expertise, you need to use the TextArea element.

Button

This element creates a button which when clicked, performs some action.

Select

Though not needed in forms where the user has to type his details, knowing about this element makes it easier for your visitors. Select element creates a drop-down list, from which the visitor can select one option.

Legend

An important element you should consider if you want your form to look organized, the legend creates a caption for the fieldset tag element which groups together related fields in the form.

HTML5 elements

These are elements unique to HTML5, and cannot be used elsewhere.

Datalist

When you want the user to get a list of options as soon as he starts typing, then Datalist can be used. This is different from the Select element, where the user can only select from a list of options. The Datalist element displays a list if the user clicks the arrow mark, and also displays the relevant choice as soon as the user starts typing.

Keygen

When you want to create a secure way to authenticate users, then the keygen element can be used. It creates 2 keys, out of which one is stored locally (the private key) and the other is sent to the server (the public key).

This list covers some of the most commonly used HTML form elements, and there are lots more to experiment with.

Try these out first, and then start experimenting with different elements! Below are some example codes that you can use, or modify to suit your needs. The <form> tag has to be used to use the form elements in your webpage. Compared to elements, there are several times more attributes, so most of the commonly used attributes will be explained after the corresponding codes.

Form Action

Before we head onto the example codes, there's one form attribute which you *must* know about, which is the "**form action**". This attribute decides which the page the data entered should be sent to, as soon as the submit button is pressed. It is here where the input gets processed. By processing, what is meant is that you can either display the details to the user, or just send it to a MySQL database, where it can be stored for future use. However, using form action requires you have to prior knowledge of ASP or PHP scripts. Since this book focuses on HTML alone, ASP and PHP will not be discussed here. There are several tutorials online that explain PHP and ASP in detail. It's not really all that difficult to understand, and you have to know about it, or HTML forms become useless since you need to send the details obtained from the user to a form handler in order to actually have some use for them.

When it comes to the syntax of the form action, it's quite simple:

<form action="page.php" method="method_you_want">

Get and Post

Now this is pretty straightforward. The page.php refers to the page you want to send the details to. If you do not have a page defined previously, then all you will get is a 'File not found' message, since no such file exists. However, if you look at the URL or go through the information provided in the File not found message, you will notice that the details that the user had entered appear explicitly. This brings us to the method used in the form action.

There are two form actions, GET and POST. If no option is selected in the beginning, then the GET option is set as default. The problem with GET is that whatever detail the user inputs, it gets displayed in the URL. While this may not pose a problem when the user is at home, imagine a scenario when he or she uses your form to enter details in a public place, or on a computer that's common to all. A small history check will open up the previously visited websites, along with the passwords and usernames in the URL. This is a huge security threat, which movies this guide toward the POST method.

In the POST method, the same action occurs - that is, the details get sent to the PHP or ASP script or a page where the details get processed - but nothing appears on the URL except the page that the form action sends the details to.

If you want to use the POST method, use the following syntax:

<form action="page.php" method="POST">

and that's it! You've now successfully created a form which gives more priority to security.

Name attribute

As you go through the examples given below, you will notice in several of the codes the attribute 'name'. This is different from the 'value' attribute, which changes the name of the displayed element - that is, the text that the user sees. The 'name' attribute works in conjunction with the form action, and it creates a variable with whatever text you have given as the identification of the variable. For example, if you give 'name="user"' right after some form input type, then that detail will get stored in a variable called 'user', which will be sent to the page you have created using the form action. In the page, you can process it by using the variable 'user' whenever you feel the need to use the corresponding detail for something.

Usually, when you want your users to submit a list of fields using just a single submit button, it becomes necessary to add the name attribute. If you fail to do so, the information will not get sent to the page, and if you include the attribute for only a couple of fields, then only those corresponding fields' details will be sent to the page for further processing.

Option tag

Before we head on to the input types and the various elements you are going to be using in a form to make it easy to use, you need to know about an important tag called the <option> tag. When you want the user to be able to select from a list of options, then this tag should be used. Let us a take a look at the syntax that is used for the option tag:

<option value="game1" Super Mario>

<option value="game2" Runescape>

If you execute this code, you will notice that all you get on your screen are the names Super Mario and Runescape, with no option to select them. The option tag only creates the options, it does nothing in grouping them into a single field. That is where the select and datalist element come in. The option tag works in conjunction with these tags, but more on these two new tags later.

For now, it is enough if you understand these basic tags and attributes, which will be used regularly in the following examples for the different elements. Let us now head on to different input types and an example code for each of them for your better understanding.

Input

There are a number of input element types. You will be making use of more than a few of them in every form that you create. Let us take a look at the basic syntax that is used for such input types:

<input type="relevant_type" name="relevant_name" value="relevant_value">

Text

This enables a single line input field (note that this field accepts only text).

Example

```
<!DOCTYPE html>

<html>

<body>

<form action="">
```

```
Username:<input type="text" name="username">

</form>

</body>

</html>
```

This code accepts text from the user when he gives his Username. The input from the user gets stored in a variable called username in the page you're sending the file to. The form action has been left blank, and you can insert whichever page you want the information to be sent to.

Submit

This creates a button called "Submit" which does exactly as it sounds. It sends the details that are entered to form handler, a fancy name for the form action.

Example

```
<form action="action.php">

  Username:<br>

  <input type="text" name="userid"><br>

  Password:<br>

  <input type="password" name="pass"><br>
```

```
<input type="submit" value="Submit">
```

```
</form>
```

Here, another input type called Password is used. When the <input type="password"> is given, the text box accepts special characters as well, and the details would be sent to the form handler as soon as the Submit button is pressed. By changing the value of the submit button, you can change the text. For example, giving 'value="Click to confirm"' will create a button that says "Click to confirm", but performs the action of the submit button.

Radio

The radio input type gives a list of choices the user can choose from, wherein he can select only one choice at any given time.

Example

```
<form>
```

```
<input          type="radio"          name="occupation"
value="student"> Student<br>
```

```
<input          type="radio"          name="occupation"
value="unemployed"> Unemployed<br>
```

```
<input type="radio" name="occupation" value="teacher">
```
Teacher

```
</form>
```

This creates a list of options regarding the user's occupation. If you want a particular choice to be selected by default, you can do that by adding a "checked" at the end of the input type.

For example, replacing "`<input type="radio" name="occupation" value="student">`" Student
 - with "`<input type="radio" name="occupation" value="student"` **checked**> Student
" will select Student by default.

Checkbox

When you want to let your user select multiple options from the choices you provide, use checkboxes. The syntax is the same as the other input types.

Example

```
<form action="action_page.php">
```

```
<input type="checkbox" name="gadget1" value="Laptop" >I have a laptop <br>
```

```
<input type="checkbox" name="gadget2" value="PC">I have a PC<br>
```

```
<input type="submit">

</form>
```

This example creates 2 checkboxes, which ask the user if he owns a laptop and a PC. Once again, if you want certain options to be selected by default, add a "checked" at the end of the input type like this:

```
<input type="checkbox" name="gadget1" value="Laptop" checked>I have a laptop <br>
```

Button

You can make use of the button input type to define the action that clicking on a button performs.

Example

```
<input type="button" onclick="alert('HTML form tutorial!')" value="Click Here Please!">
```

This small code generates a button which says "Click Here Please!", which when clicked pops a message up saying "HTML form tutorial". As with the other input types, changing the value will change the message displayed inside the button.

Number

This is an input type which will accept only numbers from the user. You can select the range of the numbers, and your user will be able to give an input which contains a number that only exists within the range. This is useful when you want to give an input field for something like birthdates, or age. The field automatically comes with selection arrows, which can be used or the user can manually type the input themselves.

Example

```
<!DOCTYPE html>

<html>

<body>

<form action="page.php">

 Birthdate:

 <input    type="number"    name="quantity"    min="1"
max="31">

 <input type="submit" value="Confirm">

</form>

</body>
```

```
</html>
```

This example code will create an input field for birthdate, with a maximum value of 31 and a minimum value of 1. You can obviously change these numbers to your liking. The keywords 'min' and 'max' stand for minimum and maximum respectively as you can probably guess. However, if your browser is Internet Explorer 9 or earlier this input type will not work.

TextArea

When your form requires your users to enter personal details, you want to have an input field which can accept more than one line of input. In such a case, using the input type text would not work, and you need to use TextArea.

Example

```
<!DOCTYPE html>

<html>

<body>

<textarea rows="5" cols="75">
```

You can use this space to type whatever you want. All of this will be displayed in the text field. If you decide to not give information or text that appears by default, you can leave this space blank, and the user will be able to enter his or her personal details or the relevant detail you want.

</textarea>

</body>

</html>

This example code unfortunately only gets the details, but does not do anything with the details. In order to process the information, you need to include a submit input type, which was discussed earlier, and a form action. This form action has to send the details to a relevant page on the website (usually within the webpage itself), where the details can be processed, and the final result can be used. For example, if you want the details to get stored in a database, you need to do so via the form action, which is not possible without a submit button. Once again, it's quite obvious, but 'rows' stands for the number of rows you want the input field to have, and 'cols' stands for the number of columns that you want (which is basically the number letters per line, including blank spaces).

Range

You may have seen in several HTML forms a slider, in which you lick on a circular button and drag it to the position you want to indicate a number or percentage. You can do that with the help of the <range> tag. This creates a slider with the minimum and maximum values set by you, that the user can use.

```
<!DOCTYPE html>

<html>

<body>

<form action="action_page.php" method="get">

Percentage:

<input type="range" name="percent" min="0" max="100">

<input type="submit">

</form>

</body>

</html>
```

This would create a slider with a range of 0-100%, and you will be able to select any value in between. This accepts only whole numbers however. An ideal example of this would in a form that gets input from the user regarding their fat percentage, height, and weight, and then give the Body Mass

Index (BMI) as an output. Here, instead of getting the input from the user as a numbers for the fat percentage, you can use a slider to do so. In the end, what matters is that the form is easy to use, and not how the input is obtained.

Note that the <range> tag is not supported in Internet Explorer 9 and its previous versions.

Time and Week

The time and week tags allow the user to input the time and week, as well as year. If your form requires your user to input his or her birth year, then using these tags will make it much easier, since it pops up a time or a week picker, from which the user can just select the time, week, and year instead of typing it out.

Example

<!DOCTYPE html>

<html>

<body>

<form action="page.php">

Choose time:

<input type="time" name="time">

```
<input type="submit">

</form>

</body>

</html>
```

This example creates a field where the user has to type in the time, or select from a time-picker which should pop up as soon as he or she starts typing. It's important to know that this time picker might not be supported in certain browsers, so do make sure to check beforehand if what you need your user to do is select from the picker and not type the input out.

In a similar way, the input type week, datetime and month can be used. Week and month work with most browsers, but datetime tag also gives the timezone. If you only want the local time in the user's country, then using datetime-local would be more appropriate. Once again, the code for datetime-local is the same as the ones for week and month.

These are some of the various input types that you can use (and will be using) in all of your forms. Now that you have a clear idea of the different input types in your mind, it is time to move onto the different elements that you can use within these input types, to make your form look even better and make it easy to use.

Select

The select attribute of the HTML form creates a drop down list. This list contains options that the user can select. This is different from the attributes like 'Number', because the user will only be able to select the option, and cannot type anything in it.

Example

<!DOCTYPE html>

<html>

<body>

<form action="page.asp" method="POST">

 Username:<input type="text" name="userid">

 <input type="submit" value="Store User ID">

List:

<select>

 <option value="a">A</option>

```
<option value="b">B</option>

<option value="c">C</option>

<option value="d">D</option>

</select>

</form>

</body>

</html>
```

Here, the POST method is used, which as stated before, will prevent the details from appearing in the URL when the user hits the submit button. In the list, you can add as many options as you want, but make sure to include the </option> tag after each option. When you want the selected option to have a specific variable name in the page you're sending it to, then use the 'name' attribute. Your code should look something like this:

```
<select name="name_you_want_in_page">
```

FieldSet and Legend

Legend is used to give a caption to the <fieldset> tag. The **Fieldset** tag groups together the elements you want. A visible border appears around the elements when the

Fieldset tag is used. This makes it much easier for your user to read and understand what is required as an input. What the legend tag does is, it creates a caption just at the top of the fieldset, which makes it even more easier for the users. As a website designer, the user's comfortability should be your primary aim, and as such, these tags will come handy.

Example

```
<!DOCTYPE html>

<html>

<body>

<form>

<fieldset>

<legend>Education:</legend>

School: <input type="text"><br>

College: <input type="text"><br>

Further qualifications: <input type="text">

<input type="submit">

</fieldset>

</form>
```

```
</body>

</html>
```

This code will create 3 text boxes, where the user will enter the corresponding details, and the submit given at the end will create a Submit button which performs the same action as stated before.

HTML5 Elements

The elements given below are but two of the various elements that have been added in HTML5. These elements work *only* in HTML5, and are not supported by previous versions.

Datalist

At times, going through a list while looking for a particular option can be quite annoying, especially if the list is very large. In such cases, adding a datalist instead of just the <option> tag would make it easier for the users. Datalist is different from the option tag, because the user can actually type the input in the field you have provided. As soon as he or she starts typing, the relevant choice pops up. You will notice that the Datalist is quite similar the number tag, only this for text. It acts as an auto-fill feature for the input field.

Example

```
<!DOCTYPE html>

<html>

<body>

<form action="page.asp" method="get">

 <input list="bike" name="bike">

 <datalist id="bike">

  <option value="bike1">

  <option value="bike2">

  <option value="bike3">

  <option value="bike4">

  <option value="bike5">

 </datalist>

 <input type="submit">

</body>

</html>
```

Despite being very useful, the datalist tag can be used only in HTML5, and is not supported by Internet Explorer 9 or its previous versions and is not supported even by Safari.

Keygen

When you want to authenticate your users, then you have to use the keygen tag. This tag does the function of creating a pair of keys. One of these keys will be stored locally, and the other will be sent to the server. Of course, the locally stored key will be private, and the other will be public.

```
<!DOCTYPE html>

<html>

<body>

<form action="page" method="get">

Username: <input type="text" name="userid">

Encryption: <keygen name="password">

<input type="submit">

</form>

</body>

</html>
```

Here, the name 'password' refers to the name of the variable in the page you're sending, which stores the generated key. Unfortunately, this tag is not supported by any of the Internet Explorer versions, so use caution before actually implementing it in your website.

This covers most of the commonly used basic elements in HTML forms that you need to know about. Remember that just reading through this will do no good; you have to actually execute these codes, experiment with them, modify them to your tastes, and finally start writing your own code in order to truly master the powerful tool that is the HTML form. This is true not only for the HTML form, but also the other elements in HTML. Now that we have seen the common elements, let us move on and take a look at some elements and attributes that can be used to make your form look a tad more organized.

Optgroup

The <optgroup> tag helps with grouping together different options. You may ask the need for grouping something that is already grouped together within a single field (usually using <select> or <datalist>. To clear this confusion, let us look at an example:

Suppose you want your user to tell what model of laptop he or she is using currently. You could just simply create a huge list of different brands of laptops with their several models. Though this it is possible, it is extremely time consuming for the user to select the laptop model from the list that contains thousands of options. Now if you did not use <datalist> but used <select>, this makes it almost impossible for the user to find his or her model, as the user will not be able to even type the first few numbers or letters, to simplify the search. This would be a code that produces results, albeit ineffectively. The very idea idea of coding is to optimize time consumed, both by the user, and by the processing.

This is where the <optgroup> tag comes into play. Suppose you group together different models under the same brand, you will be able to create a list which contains the brand names, with a sub-list in between each brand name which would contain the model. Not only will this make the selection process much easier for the user, it also organizes your list, giving it a more professional and presentable look.

Example

<!DOCTYPE html>

<html>

<body>

```
<select>

  <optgroup label="HP">

   <option value="envy">Envy</option>

   <option value="pavilion">Pavilion</option>

  </optgroup>

  <optgroup label="Lenovo">

   <option value="y50">Y50</option>

   <option value="y40">Y40</option>

  </optgroup>

</select>

</body>

</html>
```

Try executing the above code without the <optgroup> tags. You will notice a list that contains Envy, Pavilion, Y50, and Y40, with no order. Now use the exact code given above, and you will obtain a list that has several sub-headings (you get the same number of sub-headings as the <optgroup> tags used) under which the models will be listed. If you are using the <select> tag to get some input from the user, and your options are quite large in number, then you *must* use the <optgroup> tag.

The 'label' in the <optgroup> syntax is the name you want to give the sub-heading. Note that only the options can be selected, and the sub-headings cannot.

Readonly

Sometimes you require a field which has a set value or text in it, which the user should not be able to change, but should be able to see. When you have such a situation in your hands, the **<readonly>** attribute becomes useful. Just as the name suggests, the user will be able to only read what is given in the field, and will not be able to make changes to the field.

The syntax for <readonly> tag is:

<input   type="type_you_need"   name="name" value="value" readonly>

Example

<!DOCTYPE html>

<html>

<body>

<form action="page.php">

Your current location:

```
<input   type="text"   name="place"   value="California"
readonly>
```

```
<br>
```

```
</form>
```

```
</body>
```

```
</html>
```

When this code gets executed, you will be able to see 'California' displayed in the input field, but will not be able to make any change to the field.

Autocomplete

An element you should definitely be aware of to make things easier for your user, especially if you form is to be used repeatedly. If your user has to submit a report once in a couple of days using your HTML form, then using the <autocomplete> tag will make it much easier for him or her. If you're aware of the Autofill setting in the Google Chrome browser, then understanding the function of this tag should be easy. It is the same, except that the user has to first input the details at least once, before the form starts autocompleting the fields.

Let us look at the basic syntax for autocomplete, which is usually placed along with the form action. This enables the autocomplete attribute in all of the form's elements.

```
<form action="page.pgp" autocomplete="on">
```

Example

```
<!DOCTYPE html>

<html>

<body>

<form action="action_page.php" autocomplete="on">

Name:<input type="text" name="name"><br>

Age:<input type="number" name="age"><br>

Work ID <input type="number" name="id" autocomplete="off"><br>

 <input type="submit">

</form>

</body>

</html>
```

This code will create 3 fields, one each for name, age and work ID. The first time the user uses the form, he or she will have to type in the details completely. From then on, whenever the form is used, autocomplete will kick in as soon as the field is double-clicked, or the first letter is typed, making everything so much more easier for the user.

Note that autocomplete is switched off for the Work ID. This is done because the Work ID, which should be kept private should not be displayed to others who type in someone else's name. What this basically means is that you can switch autocomplete attribute off to which field you want by adding an <autocomplete="off"> at the end of the input type.

This covers most of the HTML form elements, and you should be able to create your own form with different elements and attributes now. Always remember to keep trying different elements to find out what makes the form easy to use. The ultimate aim of a form is to make it easy to use so that even a layman will be able fill it up quickly.

Chapter 8
HTML Images

Images can be very helpful to beautify and to explain the complex concepts of your web page in a simple way. In this chapter, we will add images to your webpages in simple steps.

Insert Image

In HTML, you can add any image to your web page with the **<img>** tag. The syntax for using the **<img>** tag is given below.

Syntax:

<img src="Image URL" ... attributes-list/>

The <img> tag is an empty one, it means that there will be no closing tag for it. You can only give the list of attributes to this tag. Here is an example.

Example

For trying the below example, you need to keep the .htm file and the image within the same directory.

```
<!DOCTYPE html> <html> <head> <title>Using Image
in Webpage</title> </head> <body> <p>Simple Image
Insert</p> <img src="/html/images/test.png" alt="Test
Image" /> </body> </html>
```

The above code will produce an output with the image used.

Simple Image Insert

HTML supports image formats like JPEG, PNG or GIF. You can use any of these image formats basing on your comfort. You should always ensure that you specify the correct file name of the image in **src** attribute. Always remember that the image names are case sensitive.

There is a mandatory attribute called the **alt** attribute, which will specify an alternate text for the image, in cases where the image fails to be displayed.

Set Image Location

It is recommended that you keep your images in a specific directory separately. We will put our .htm file in the home directory and the images in a subdirectory called **images,** within the home directory. Here is an example.

Example

Here, we will assume the image location to be "/html/image/test.png", for this example.

```
<!DOCTYPE html> <html> <head> <title>Using Image
in Webpage</title> </head> <body> <p>Simple Image
Insert</p> <img src="/html/images/test.png" alt="Test
Image" /> </body> </html>
```

The above code will produce an output with the specified image.

Set Image Width/Height

Depending on your requirements, you can set the height and width of an image with the help of the **height** and **width** attributes. The height and width for the image can either be specified in terms of its percentage with its actual size or in terms of pixels. Not that the original resolution of the image will change if the ratios are not maintained. Here is an example.

Example

```
<!DOCTYPE html> <html> <head> <title>Set Image
Width and Height</title> </head> <body> <p>Setting
image          width          and          height</p> <img
```

src="/html/images/test.png" alt="Test Image" width="200" height="150"/> </body> </html>

The above code will produce an output image with the width 200 and height 150.

Set Image Border

Every image by default will have a border surrounding it. You can specify the thickness of the border using the **border** attribute, in terms of pixels. If you wish to remove the border around your image, you should set the thickness to 0. Here is an example.

Example

<!DOCTYPE html> <html> <head> <title>Set Image Border</title> </head> <body> <p>Setting image Border</p> <img src="/html/images/test.png" alt="Test Image" border="3"/> </body> </html>

The above code will produce an output with the border 3.

Set Image Alignment

All the images, by default, will be aligned to the left. You can specify the alignment of the image using the **align** attribute to set the image to the right or center. Here is an example.

Example

```
<!DOCTYPE html> <html> <head> <title>Set Image
Alignment</title> </head> <body> <p>Setting image
Alignment</p> <img src="/html/images/test.png"
alt="Test Image" border="3"
align="right"/> </body> </html>
```

The above code will produce an output image aligned to the right, with a border 3.

Chapter 9

HTML Lists

In HTML, information can be specified using three types of lists. A list must contain at least one list element. Lists contain:

<ul> - This is an unordered list. The list items will be listed using plain bullets.

<ol> - This is an ordered list. The list items in this list will be listed with different schemes of numbers.

<dl> - This is a definition list. The items in the definition list will be arranged in the same way as they are in a dictionary.

HTML Unordered Lists

And unordered list can be defined as a collection of items with no special sequence or order. You can create this list by using the <ul> tag. All the items in this list will be marked using bullets. Here is an example.

Example

```
<!DOCTYPE html> <html> <head> <title>HTML
Unordered List</title> </head> <body> <ul> <li>Apple</li> <li>
Mango</li> <li>Banana</li> <li>Pear</li> </ul> </body> </html>
```

The above code will produce the following output:

Apple

Mango

Banana

Pear

The type Attribute

You can actually specify the type of bullet to be used by using the **type** attribute of the <ul> tag. The default a bullet time is a disc. The other possible options are:

```
<ul type="disc">
```

```
<ul type="square">
```

```
<ul type="circle">
```

Example

Following is an example where we used <ul type="square">

```
<!DOCTYPE           html> <html> <head> <title>HTML
Unordered              List</title> </head> <body>   <ul
type="square">   <li>Apple</li>   <li>Mango</li>   <li>
Banana</li>   <li>Pear</li>   </ul> </body> </html>
```

The above code will produce the following output:

Apple

Mango

Banana

Pear

Example

Following is an example where we used <ul type="disc"> :

```
<!DOCTYPE           html> <html> <head> <title>HTML
Unordered              List</title> </head> <body>   <ul
type="disc">   <li>Apple</li>   <li>Mango</li>   <li>Ba
nana</li>   <li>Pear</li>   </ul> </body> </html>
```

The above code will produce the following output:

Apple

Mango

Banana

Pear

Example

Following is an example where we used <ul type="circle"> :

<!DOCTYPE html> <html> <head> <title>HTML Unordered List</title> </head> <body> <ul type="circle"> <li>Apple</li> <li>Mango</li> <li>B anana</li> <li>Pear</li> </ul> </body> </html>

The above code will produce the following output:

Apple

Mango

Banana

Pear

HTML Ordered Lists

You can use the order list in HTML when you are required to place the list items in a numbered list, instead of using the regular bulleted list. You can place the items in an ordered list by using the **<ol>** tag. The number in for an ordered list starts with 1 and it will be incremented by 1 with each element added to this list using <li>. Here is an example.

Example

<!DOCTYPE html> <html> <head> <title>HTML Ordered List</title> </head> <body> <ol> <li>Apple</li> <li> Mango</li> <li>Banana</li> <li>Pear</li> </ol> </body> </html>

The above code will produce the following output:

Apple

Mango

Banana

Pear

The type Attribute

You can specify the numbering type you like by using the **type** attribute of the <ol> tag. The number will be the default numbering type. The other possible options are the following:

<ol type="A"> - Upper-Case Letters.

<ol type="a"> - Lower-Case Letters.

<ol type="I"> - Upper-Case Numerals.

<ol type="i"> - Lowercase Numerals.

<ol type="1"> - Default-Case Numerals.

Example

We will use the <ol type="1"> for this example.

```
<!DOCTYPE html> <html> <head> <title>HTML
Ordered List</title> </head> <body> <ol
type="1"> <li>Apple</li> <li>Mango</li> <li>Banan
a</li> <li>Pear</li> </ol> </body> </html>
```

The above code will produce the following output:

Apple

Mango

Banana

Pear

Example

We will use the <ol type="I"> for this example.

```
<!DOCTYPE          html> <html> <head> <title>HTML
Ordered              List</title> </head> <body>  <ol
type="I">  <li>Apple</li>  <li>Mango</li>  <li>Banan
a</li>  <li>Pear</li>  </ol> </body> </html>
```

The above code will produce the following output:

Apple

Mango

Banana

Pear

Example

We will use the <ol type="i"> for this example.

```
<!DOCTYPE          html> <html> <head> <title>HTML
Ordered              List</title> </head> <body>  <ol
type="i">  <li>Apple</li>  <li>Mango</li>  <li>Banan
a</li>  <li>Pear</li>  </ol> </body> </html>
```

The above code will produce the following output:

Apple

Mango

Banana

Pear

Example

We will use the <ol type="A"> for this example.

```
<!DOCTYPE html> <html> <head> <title>HTML Ordered List</title> </head> <body> <ol type="A"> <li>Apple</li> <li>Mango</li> <li>Banana</li> <li>Pear</li> </ol> </body> </html>
```

The above code will produce the following output:

Apple

Mango

Banana

Pear

Example

We will use the <ol type="a"> for this example.

```
<!DOCTYPE html> <html> <head> <title>HTML Ordered List</title> </head> <body> <ol type="a"> <li>Apple</li> <li>Mango</li> <li>Banana</li> <li>Pear</li> </ol> </body> </html>
```

The above code will produce the following output:

Apple

Mango

Banana

Pear

The start Attribute

You can specify the starting point with a specific number to start a list with the help of the **start** attribute of the <ol> tag. The other possible options the following (we will start at the numbering with 3).

<ol type="1" start="3">   - Numerals starts with 3

<ol type="a" start="3">   - Letters starts with c

<ol type="A" start="3">   - Letters starts with C

<ol type="i" start="3">   - Numerals starts with iii

<ol type="I" start="3">   - Numerals starts with III

Example

Following is an example where we used <ol type="i" start="3" >

```
<!DOCTYPE        html> <html> <head> <title>HTML
Ordered    List</title> </head> <body>  <ol    type="i"
start="3">   <li>Apple</li>   <li>Mango</li>   <li>Bana
na</li>   <li>Pear</li>   </ol> </body> </html>
```

The above code will produce the following output:

Apple

Mango

Banana

Pear

HTML Definition Lists

XHTML an HDMI support a list style called the **definition
list.** Here are the entities will be listed like as they are in a
encyclopaedia or dictionary. Using the definition list is ideal
for representing a list of items, glossary, or other
value/name lists.

The given tags will be used by the definition list.

<dl> - Defines the start of the list

<dt> - A term

<dd> - Term definition

\</dl\> - Defines the end of the list

Here is an example using \<dt\>

Example

\<!DOCTYPE html\> \<html\> \<head\> \<title\>HTML Definition List\</title\> \</head\> \<body\> \<dl\> \<dt\>\<b\>HTML\</b\> \</dt\> \<dd\>This stands for Hyper Text Markup Language\</dd\> \<dt\>\<b\>HTTP\</b\>\</dt\> \<dd\>This stands for Hyper Text Transfer Protocol\</dd\> \</dl\> \</body\> \</html\>

The above code will produce the following output:

HTML

This stands for Hyper Text Markup Language

HTTP

This stands for Hyper Text Transfer Protocol

Chapter 10
HTML Colors

Colors play a very important role in beautifying your web page, making it good to look and feel it. On the page level, you can specify the colors by using the <body> tag. You can also use the **bgcolor** attribute for setting the colors what different tags.

The following attributes are available with the <body> tag, with which different colors can be set.

vlink - This will set the color for the links that are visited (links clicked once or more)

link - The color of the linked text can be set using this.

alink - The color for the selected links or active links can be set using this.

text - The body text color can be set with this.

bgcolor - The color of the background can be set with this.

HTML Color Coding Methods

There are three different methods in HTML for setting setting colors for the web page. They are as follows:

Color names - you can directly specify the names of the colors like red, blue or green.

Hex codes - You can specify the color using a six digit hex code. Every color can be represented by the red, blue and green colors present in them. The hex code is nothing but a representation of this.

Color decimal or percentage values - This value will be specified by using the rgb( ) property.

Now we will have a look at these coloring schemes in detail.

HTML Colors - Color Names

You can directly specify the name of the color for setting it as the background or text color. There are a total of 16 basic colors listed by W3C, that validate with the HTML validator. Most of the major browsers support more than 200 different colors.

W3C Standard 16 Colors

The list of 16 standard colors, recommended by W3C is given below.

Black	Gray	Silver	White
Yellow	Lime	Aqua	Fuchsia
Red	Green	Blue	Purple
Maroon	Olive	Navy	Teal

Example

Here is an example where we said to the background color using the color name.

<!DOCTYPE html> <html> <head> <title>HTML Colors by Name</title> </head> <body text="blue" bgcolor="green"> <p>Use different color names for for body and table and see the result.</p> <table bgcolor="black"> <tr> <td> <font color="white">This text will appear white on black background.</font> </td> </tr> </table> </body> </html>

HTML Colors - Hex Codes

The hex code is nothing but the six digit the presentation for a color. The first two digits of the hex code represent the value of red, the next two digits represented the value of green and the last two digits represented the value of blue. The hex code will be RRGGBB.

You can take the hexadecimal value from graphics software like MS paint, Paintshop Pro or Adobe Photoshop.

A hash sign # or pound will precede the hexadecimal code. Given below is a table with the colors using hex code.

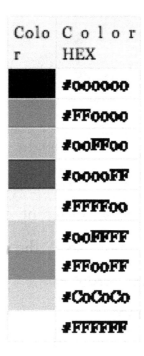

Color	Color HEX
	#000000
	#FF0000
	#00FF00
	#0000FF
	#FFFF00
	#00FFFF
	#FF00FF
	#C0C0C0
	#FFFFFF

Example

Here are the examples to set background of an HTML tag by color code in hexadecimal:

<!DOCTYPE html> <html> <head> <title>HTML Colors by Hex</title> </head> <body text="#0000FF"

bgcolor="#00FF00"> <p>Use different color hex for for body and table and see the result.</p> <table bgcolor="#000000"> <tr> <td> <font color="#FFFFFF">This text will appear white on black background.</font> </td> </tr> </table> </body> </html>

HTML Colors - RGB Values

The color value can be specified with the **rgb( )** property. This takes 3 values as the input for the colors red, green and blue, respectively. The range of each color varies from integer values 0 to 255 or as a percentage.

The list of the RGB values for few colors is given below.

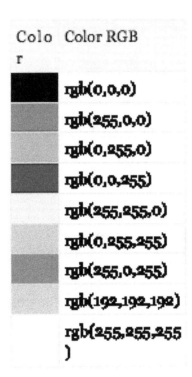

Color	Color RGB
	rgb(0,0,0)
	rgb(255,0,0)
	rgb(0,255,0)
	rgb(0,0,255)
	rgb(255,255,0)
	rgb(0,255,255)
	rgb(255,0,255)
	rgb(192,192,192)
	rgb(255,255,255)

Example

Here are the examples to set background of an HTML tag by color code using rgb() values:

<!DOCTYPE html> <html> <head> <title>HTML Colors by RGB code</title> </head> <body text="rgb(0,0,255)" bgcolor="rgb(0,255,0)"> <p>Use different color code for for body and table and see the result.</p> <table bgcolor="rgb(0,0,0)"> <tr> <td> <font color="rgb(255,255,255)">This text will appear white on black

background.</font> </td> </tr> </table> </body> </html>

Note: Not all browsers support the rgb() color property. You should be careful on its usage for this reason.

Browser Safe Colors

There are a total of 216 colors that are supposed to be browser safe. They are computer independent colors. These colors range from the 000000 to FFFFFF in hex code. All computers having the 256 color palette support these.

			000099	0000CC	0000FF
		003366	003399	0033CC	0033FF
006600	006633	006666	006699	0066CC	0066FF
009900	009933	009966	009999	0099CC	0099FF
00CC00	00CC33	00CC66	00CC99	00CCCC	00CCFF
00FF00	00FF33	00FF66	00FF99	00FFCC	00FFFF
			330099	3300CC	3300FF
333300	333333	333366	333399	3333CC	3333FF
336600	336633	336666	336699	3366CC	3366FF
339900	339933	339966	339999	3399CC	3399FF
33CC00	33CC33	33CC66	33CC99	33CCCC	33CCFF
33FF00	33FF33	33FF66	33FF99	33FFCC	33FFFF
		660066	660099	6600CC	6600FF
663300	663333	663366	663399	6633CC	6633FF
666600	666633	666666	666699	6666CC	6666FF
669900	669933	669966	669999	6699CC	6699FF
66CC00	66CC33	66CC66	66CC99	66CCCC	66CCFF
66FF00	66FF33	66FF66	66FF99	66FFCC	66FFFF
990000	990033	990066	990099	9900CC	9900FF
993300	993333	993366	993399	9933CC	9933FF
996600	996633	996666	996699	9966CC	9966FF
999900	999933	999966	999999	9999CC	9999FF
99CC00	99CC33	99CC66	99CC99	99CCCC	99CCFF
99FF00	99FF33	99FF66	99FF99	99FFCC	99FFFF
CC0000	CC0033	CC0066	CC0099	CC00CC	CC00FF
CC3300	CC3333	CC3366	CC3399	CC33CC	CC33FF
CC6600	CC6633	CC6666	CC6699	CC66CC	CC66FF
CC9900	CC9933	CC9966	CC9999	CC99CC	CC99FF
CCCC00	CCCC33	CCCC66	CCCC99	CCCCCC	CCCCFF
CCFF00	CCFF33	CCFF66	CCFF99	CCFFCC	CCFFFF
FF0000	FF0033	FF0066	FF0099	FF00CC	FF00FF
FF3300	FF3333	FF3366	FF3399	FF33CC	FF33FF
FF6600	FF6633	FF6666	FF6699	FF66CC	FF66FF
FF9900	FF9933	FF9966	FF9999	FF99CC	FF99FF
FFCC00	FFCC33	FFCC66	FFCC99	FFCCCC	FFCCFF
FFFF00	FFFF33	FFFF66	FFFF99	FFFFCC	FFFFFF

Chapter 11
HTML Multimedia

With multimedia being the rage these days in the Internet, there are no designers in the world today who do not want to add multimedia to their websites. Adding multimedia ensures that your website looks stunning, and if your website requires a steady flow of traffic, then adding such media becomes a necessity.

When the first browsers were launched, they supported only text. Can you imagine a webpage displaying nothing but text? No pictures, no videos, no sounds, no gifs. The worst part was that only one font and one color existed! Sounds dull and boring, doesn't it? Which is exactly what must have been going through the minds of the browser developers at that time, because the browsers which came up after that started supporting media!

Adding multimedia is very easy and fun to do, but it lies up to you to figure out if the browser - which your users will be using - will support the media or not. Most browsers support the popular formats discussed in this chapter, but sometimes, it will not work. In these not-so-rare cases, you might need to install an additional programs (called a plug-in) to let the media work in the web browser. Fortunately, with HTML5, all these problems will disappear, and a promising future for multimedia lies ahead.

Since adding images has already been discussed previously, this chapter will focus specifically on integrating videos and sounds into your webpage. While you do this, it is your responsibility to make the perusal of your webpage by your users as easy as possible. What this means is that you have to be able to decide if you want some images and sounds to play automatically as soon as a page pops up. If your website targets users who are well off, they most likely will be having a fast internet connection, which means loading these images and sounds will not waste their time. Imagine a person with really slow connection. If you start adding sounds and images to your webpages to be loaded as soon as the page is opened, the user will never be able to use your site properly because of the slow connection. It's a tradeoff, between making your webpage really attractive and catchy, and maintaining your user-base. This is a serious issue when your website is one that earns money from the traffic it gets. Maintaining your user-base is more important than adding loads of media into your webpage, especially if your website doesn't revolve around the topic of multimedia.

With the unfortunately boring, but serious issue out of the way and your decision in the tradeoff having been made, let us take a look at some popular video and sound formats that are most commonly used these days, along with some example codes on how to add them into your website.

MPEG

Developed by Moving Pictures Experts Group, the MPEG format became the rage on the internet as soon as it came into existence. The most popular format up to date, it's supported by every browser out there. That's right, every single one of them! Unfortunately, being very picky, HTML5 allows only a few video formats, namely the MP4, WebM and Ogg. As such, this format will not be discussed here.

In previous versions of HTML, you are required to install an additional plug-in in order to embed videos on to your webpage. As tedious as it sounds, it was actually how things were done before. But now, with HTML5, this problem has been solved, and videos can now be included with just a simple **<video>** tag, much like how the HTML supports images using <img> tag (as discussed in an earlier chapter).

Adding Videos

The basic syntax for adding videos is :

<video>

<source>

</video>

Now, the source tag obviously should not be blank as given above. Let us take a look at an example, and then we will see the different attributes used, and which attributes you *can* use to further customize the video appearance on the web page.

Example

```
<!DOCTYPE html>

<html>

<body>

<video width="640" height="480" controls>

  <source src="example.mp4" type="example/mp4">

  <source src="example.ogg" type="example/ogg">
```

```
</video>

</body>

</html>
```

The above code will embed the example video on to the website. If it has not come to your attention yet, there are 2 videos included here. It's actually just one video in 2 different formats. The browser will automatically include the video that it supports, and disregards the other video format. Also, when you decide to include text within the video tags, it gets displayed *only* if the browser does not support the format. Therefore, a good (and easy) way of checking if the browser supports a specific format would be to try this code out first before executing your actual code:

```
<!DOCTYPE html>

<html>

<body>

<video>

 <source src="example.mp4" type="example/mp4">
```

Looks like your browser does not support the mp4 format. Try another browser, or change the format now.

```
</video>

</body>

</html>
```

The text given after the <source> tag will get displayed on your screen only when the format of the video you have taken is not supported by the browser.

Let us now take a look at the different attributes included in this example.

Width and Height

Under the <video> tag, width and height are mentioned, which are the dimensions of the video as it appears on the webpage. If you do not include the the width and height attributes, the browser will automatically select the default width to height ratio of the video. When you go for the default video size as chosen by the browser, the video will begin to flicker whenever it loads, which becomes an annoying issue.

However, if you do include these two attributes, but give lower aspect ratios than the actual video, then the video displayed on the webpage will be scaled down, proportionately. If you give the width and height attributes a value greater than the video's actual aspect ratio, then the

the video will cover more screen, but the video size remains as is. The rest of the area gets filled by a black space. For a user, this would look absolutely horrible, and you should avoid giving greater aspect ratios at all costs. When worst comes to worst and you are not able to find out the aspect ratio of the video, then just include the video without any aspect ratio. The default video size look will be much better than the same sized video being displayed in large black space.

Controls

You must have seen the play, pause, seeking, volume, toggle full-screen, captions/subtitles and other controls in most of the video streaming websites you have used. These are nothing but the 'controls' in HTML5. Instead of adding these options one by one, HTML5 makes it extremely easy; all you have to do is include the term 'controls' in the video tag, and all of these options become available in the video.

It's important to note that the the full-screen option may not be available to you if the browser does not support it. It is mandatory that you check which browser accepts the video format you are using, and which browser allows the full-screen option.

Source

Source src is literally as it sounds - this is what you have to use to specify which video you want to embed on to the website. When you include multiple source files in different formats, then the browser will automatically use the first format that it recognizes. Basically, the source attribute is your way of telling the browser to pick whatever format it wants.

Allowfullscreen

An attribute that would make users extremely happy, the allowfullscreen attribute does what it says. It gives the user a choice of using the full-screen option. Usually, when videos are played, they do not maximize automatically, and in most cases there will not be an option to play the video in the entirety of the screen since the videos are normally played within the specified iframes. However, in HTML5, the allowfullscreen attribute makes everything better by adding the full-screen feature. When the attribute is enabled, you should be able to see a full-screen button at the bottom right corner of the video, which when clicked opens the video in a fullscreen. This attribute should not really pose a problem to you, since most browsers allow fullscreen options. An important point for you to note here is that *only* if the browser used itself has a fullscreen option will the allowfullscreen attribute work.

Autoplay

This is a very dangerous attribute to experiment with. It does not really have any technical problems, but this feature can either make or break your user-base. When the <autoplay> attribute is included, the video you have embedded on to your website starts playing as soon as the page loads. While this may make it seem like you are actually doing the user a favor by automatically playing the video for him or her, if the user has a slow connection then the page will take quite a long time to load. This means that the chances of losing your users increases drastically.

To enable autoplay, just add the 'autoplay' at the end of the video tag, as shown in the following example:

<!DOCTYPE html>

<html>

<body>

<video>

  <source   src="example.mp4"   type="example/mp4" **autoplay**>

  Looks like your browser does not support the mp4 format. Try another browser, or change the format now.

```
</video>

</body>

</html>
```

This is the same code, with the addition of autoplay. If the browser supports the video format, then the video automatically plays in the webpage.

With this, we come to conclusion of the video tag being used in HTML5 to embed videos on to your webpage. Embedding videos on to your webpage has become very easy with HTML5, but do take care and ensure that the web browser your users will be using actually supports the format.

MP4, Ogg, and WebM are all together supported only by Google Chrome, Mozilla Firefox and Opera at the moment. Make sure to use these browsers, to ensure that the video you are embedding is able to be viewed on the web page.

Let us now take a look at integrating audio on to your webpage.

Adding Audio

As with videos, prior to HTML5, audio could not be integrated into a website easily. The website designer had to use additional programs called plug-ins to let the audio play in the website. That is to say, there was no standard. HTML5 once again swept away these hardships and brought us a new, easy way for playing audio files in a web page : the <audio> tag.

HTML supported different audio formats, but only with the help of the annoying plug-ins (which used to be the primary reason for the webpage crashing). HTML5 however, is picky with audio as well as video, and allows *only 3* formats. These are the ogg, mp3, and wav formats.

With these three options at hand, a question might pop in your head, asking which format should be used. All these formats pale in comparison to the size of the average video file, and you should be able to use any of them. However, audio files with the mp3 extension traditionally are bigger in size than the audio files with the ogg extension. With regards to quality, mp3 is better than ogg, but the difference in the quality is so tiny that you will not even be able to recognize it. It is safe to say that it does not really matter either way. With respect to wav however, both ogg and mp3 formats are smaller in size.

Uncompressed wav audio files are surprisingly large, but are supported by most of the browsers. Ogg has the smallest size, but it is not universal unfortunately. Several browsers do not accept ogg audio files. Therefore, mp3 audio files would be the best option to go for, as they are moderate in size, and are supported by all browsers.

Let us now take a look at an example for better understanding of how certain audio files can be added to your webpage:

```
<!DOCTYPE html>

<html>

<body>

<audio controls>

  <source src="example.ogg" type="example/ogg">

  <source src="example.mp3" type="example/mpeg">

</audio>

</body>

</html>
```

Source

The <source> part of the code does exactly the same thing as the <source> in the video section explained above. It simply tells the browser which audio file to select. If multiple formats are given, then the browser will decide to take the first format that it can support. The others would be disregarded.

Controls

The controls attribute gives the audio file on the webpage options like play, volume and pause, which are essential in any audio file.

When you are unsure of whether the browser you are using supports a particular file, try executing the follow example code:

```
<!DOCTYPE html>

<html>

<body>

<audio controls>

  <source src="example.ogg" type="example/ogg">

  <source src="example.mp3" type="example/mpeg">

Does not support, apparently.

</audio>

</body>
```

```
</html>
```

If you see the text that you have typed in above on the screen, then that means the browser does not support the format you are using. Basically, all the text within the <audio> and </audio> tags will not be displayed if the browser supports the format. The displaying of the text is a clear indication that you should either change the browser being used, or the format being used.

Embedding YouTube videos

Here is an interesting and easy way of embedding videos that are online on your website. Of course, you have to give credits to the original owners, but you *can* embed online videos. The next part of this chapter will focus on how to embed YouTube videos (the most widely used video-sharing website) on to your own website. In HTML5, you can embed videos easily, but as stated before, embedding videos and audio in HTML is very difficult, unless you just use YouTube.

To know more about embedding YouTube videos, let us first take a look and try to understand the function of a very important element in this context:

iframe

The iframe tag is used to specify an inline frame ('i' in iframe stands for inline). What this means is that you can embed another document within the document you are currently working on. This is a really easy way to embed YouTube videos on to your webpage, and is recommended.

The general syntax is:

<iframe src="document_you_want_to_add">

</iframe>

As with audio and video tags, if you want to see if your current browser supports the iframe tag, just add some text within the <iframe> and </iframe> tags. If it gets displayed on the screen, then the browser does not support the tag. If there is no text, then that means the browser is giving you the green signal to proceed.

The following steps will give you a clear idea on adding videos from YouTube to your webpage:

1. Note the video ID. When you play a video on YouTube, a unique ID is generated, which you should make a note of.

2. Create the <iframe> tag in your webpage, and make sure to include whatever height and width ratio you want in your player.

3. Within the iframe tag, let the src attribute point towards the URL of the YouTube video. This is where the video ID you took note of earlier becomes useful. And that's it! It is really simple, isn't it?

An example code is given below:

```
<!DOCTYPE html>

<html>

<body>

<iframe width="420" height="345"

src="http://www.youtube.com/embed/enter_your_video_ID_here">

</iframe>

</body>

</html>
```

Is that all you can do with YouTube videos? Definitely not! You can create playlists, make use of autohide, autoplay, controls, and loop functions that YouTube gives you permission for.

To make use of these parameters, you have to add a certain symbol after the embedded URL. At this stage, you do not really need to know what the symbol means, it is sufficient for you to just know that you have to use it. This symbol is the question mark, which should be added at the end of the URL, followed by the parameter you want to make use of. If you want to add several parameters to the same link, then you have to make use of the "&" symbol. Basically, just use the question mark for the first parameter, and then use the ampersand symbol for the other parameters.

Let us now take a look at an easy way of adding these parameters to your embedded link:

http://www.youtube.com/embed/enter_your_video_ID_here?autoplay=1

If you notice, there is a number equated to autoplay. A parameter can have different functions. For example, autoplay parameter has the capability of either playing the video by default when it is opened, or not. Thus, 0 and 1 are its values, where *autoplay=1* stands for enabling autoplay and *autoplay=0* stands for disabling autoplay. This holds true not just for autoplay, but for all the YouTube parameters. YouTube itself has defined these parameters and given them these values for the corresponding functions, so you have to stick to this format.

In a case where you want multiple parameters to be added into a single URL, then the syntax would go something like this:

http://www.youtube.com/embed/enter_your_video_ID_here?autoplay=1&controls=0

Here, the controls like play, pause and seeking will not be displayed, and the video will start playing automatically. That is what the value 0 does to the controls parameter. Now that you know about these parameters, your interest in the values of the parameters has probably piqued. Given below are some of the YouTube parameters, along with their values and their corresponding functions:

Autohide

It decides if the player controls should be displayed or not.

Value 0 makes the autohide parameter display the player control always.

Value 1 hides the player controls, as soon as the video has started playing

Value 2 lets the browser choose between 0 and 1, depending on the player size. If the player is in 16:9 or 4:3 ratio, then option 1 will be selected, otherwise, option 0 is selected. This value is selected by default.

Autoplay

Just as the name says, it decides whether the video should play as soon as the player loads or not.

Value 0 - The video will not play as soon as the player loads. The user has to click to play the video. This option is toggled by default, since the choice of watching the video should lie in the user's hands.

Value 1 - The video will play as soon as the player loads, automatically.

Loop

The loop parameter is used to decide if the video should loop and play repeatedly or not. It's never a good idea to keep a video on loop, and it would be in your best interests to select the option which disables the loop option.

Value 0 - By default, this is selected, and the video gets played only once.

Value 1 - The video keeps playing and looping forever.

Playlists

You can also create a playlist of YouTube videos. You do not need to create separate src codes, you can create a playlist using just a single source URL.

First off, note down the ID of the YouTube playlist. You need this ID so that your browser can refer to it when you embed the playlist on your webpage. Now you have to use the videoseries parameter.

An example code for embedding a playlist in your webpage would be:

http://www.youtube.com/embed/videoseries?list= ID_you_took_note_of

The method used to embed videos (iframe) here is the simplest of them all, and is highly recommended by YouTube as well. That does not necessarily mean that this is the only way of embedding videos on your webpage. Before <iframe> tag became popular, two tags were generally used: <object> and <embed> . Though deprecated from early 2015, it is still possible to use these tags, and as a website creator and designer, you need to know about using these tags as well.

Let us look at an example to further understand the syntax of the object and embed tags:

Object

Before iframe became popular, the object tag was the de facto way of embedding any video on to a web page. It worked really well, but had some serious demerits, which is why YouTube currently disapproves of using the the <object> tag to embed its videos. We will see more about about why iframe is preferred over object later on. For now, let us take a look at a small example to see how the <object> tag works:

<!DOCTYPE html>

<html>

<body>

<object width="420" height="315"

data="http://www.youtube.com/embed/**enter_the_vide o_ID_here**">

</object>

</body>

</html>

As with the <iframe> tag, the object tag also requires you to specify the width to height aspect ratio, or you will face problems as the video begins to load. A notable change with the <object> tag is that the video is specified in the **data** attribute. There is no source src attribute here. As with iframe, there are several attributes you can use with the <object> tag, but you will not be using <object> tag much, and hence it will not be discussed in detail here, but if you really want to learn about the <object> tag, there are plenty of tutorials online that will be able to answer all your queries.

Embed

Embed works the same as object does, but here (once again) the src attribute is used to point to the YouTube video. If you are using a really old browser, then chances are embed tag is the only option for you to embed videos on to your web page. Most of the very old browsers do not support the <object> tag.

Here is an example that depicts how the <embed> tag ought to be used to embed YouTube videos (or any video):

<!DOCTYPE html>

<html>

<body>

```
<embed width="420" height="315"
```

src="http://www.youtube.com/embed/**enter_video_ID _here**">

```
</body>
```

```
</html>
```

Why iframe?

With all this in mind, let us now try and understand why the <iframe> tag is *much* more widely used than the other 2 tags.

Essentially, iframe and the code embedded along with it are dynamic or 'live'. What this means is that if some changes are made either intentionally or unintentionally to the settings, the embedded code will automatically adjust itself to accommodate the new changes. For example, to let some videos run you need to have shockwave flash player installed. If the user does not have this installed, then the code automatically allows the user to view the video with the help of the plug-in or player installed in the webpage. Another advantage in using the iframe tag is the format used. Some browsers do not allow certain formats, as discussed earlier. This is especially true in HTML5, which supports only 3 formats! But when you include the same source file in different formats using the **source src** attribute in the <iframe> tag, then the browser gets the ability to automatically decide which format to play without the user or designer intervening. By default, the browser selects the first format that it recognizes and supports. While this may sound as a meagre issue to you right now, you will understand the problems behind <object> tag when you include a video file in a format that your browser does not support and end up staring at a huge blank screen, almost like the White Screen of Death).

Coming to <object> tag, the greatest drawback is that it is static. To be more accurate, the embedded code added along with the <object> tag is static. What this means it that it does not allow its code to vary according to changes made in the settings. When you use the <iframe> tag in embed your videos, you do not need to give much importance to shockwave-flash player. In stark contrast, if you decide to embed your videos using the <object> tag and do not have the required software (player) installed on your browser, all you will end up seeing is the blank screen.

In essence, it is safe to say that going the <iframe> way is best, and will work out the best results. Only in cases where <iframe> fails should you need to start using the <object> and <embed> tags.

Adding plug-ins

You may have the term 'plug-ins' used throughout this chapter. Plug-ins are nothing but small, simple helper applications that give the browser an additional function. It may be more appropriate to say that the plug-ins *extend* the functionality of a browser. There will be times when you will be expected to add a plug-in to let the browser you are using support some video or audio file. A characteristic of a good website is to have as less plug-ins as possible, however that does not mean you should not have any. Plug-ins make your task much easier, by allowing the browser to support formats that would have previously result in a white screen. Among the several hundred thousands of plug-ins available, Java applets are widely used. This is because they are easy to code, and can be coded from any platform.

Plug-ins are also the major reason why <object> and <embed> tags are used. You can add the helper application for a diverse operations. Listed below are only a few:

- Virus scans

- GPS

- Flash players

As you can see, flash players are also plug-ins. Imagine surfing the internet without adobe shockwave! Sounds ridiculous, doesn't it? This is why knowing about plug-ins and how to add them into a webpage becomes important.

To embed plug-ins, you are required to use the <object> and <embed> tags. Let us now take an example to further understand how the object tag works.

<!DOCTYPE html>

<html>

<body>

<object width="500" height="100" data="example.swf"></object>

</body>

</html>

The .swf format stands for Shockwave Flash, and it is a format that used by files that have small animations and sound. The .swf format was designed specifically with speed and efficiency in mind, and as such, using .swf formats to display small animations might be a good idea. Now, onto the attributes - **width** and **height** do the same function as explained before (they decide the object's dimensions. The

data attribute is used to specify the file you are going to be displaying, be it an audio or video file, along with the format.

This concludes the chapter on HTML multimedia. HTML5 will create new standards for multimedia, and sharing it will become easier than ever. Therefore it is imperative that you know about the basics of HTML5 as well (only after you master HTML, though).

Chapter 12
HTML5 and Semantics

Once you have truly mastered HTML, you will begin to notice that the tags you use usually make no sense, unless you know what it does. For example, consider the tag <div>. When a person who has no knowledge of HTML sees this tag, he or she will *never* be able to figure out the true meaning of the tag, or its function. This isn't really much of an issue, but it is quite annoying.

We evolved from having to use just binary numbers to using text. Why not take it a step further and use text that actually make sense to both man and machine? This is exactly what HTML5 does. With HTML5, semantic elements have been added, using which HTML coding has become extremely easy.

We have already discussed in detail about one semantic element, thought it was not mentioned at the time : <form>.

Yes, the form tag is a semantic element! When you see the tag <form>, you automatically realize it has something to do with forms, and you can start adding attributes accordingly.

Given below is a list of some of the semantic elements that HTML5 offers:

<details>

<article>

<section>

<summary>

<time>

<aside>

<mark>

We shall now proceed to look at some examples to understand how these tags work.

Article

The article tag lets you create an article. You can, of course, create an article that has some relation to the web page, but the general idea of an article is that each article should be different. Therefore, the <article> tag is used when you want to mention something that goes out of context, or is not related to the main topic of the website in the slightest.

Here is an example code which you can try out:

```
<!DOCTYPE html>

<html>

<body>

<article>

  <h2>This is the article's heading</h1>

  <p>With the help of the article tag, you can create articles that provide content not related to the webpage.</p>

</article>

</body>

</html>
```

The above code will execute the text given, with the heading in the <h2> size.

Section

Sections are groups of content that are based on a single idea or theme. This is how they differ from articles, where the theme can be anything. Sections have to stick to one theme for the word to make sense. Here is an example of how 2 sections can be put together in HTML:

```
<!DOCTYPE html>

<html>

<body>

<section>

  <h1>Section 1</h1>

  <p>This is section 1's content. This section states that HTML coding is easy to learn, and easy to forget, so stay in practice if you want to become a professional!</p>

</section>

<section>

  <h1>Section 2</h1>

  <p>This is section 2. This section would like to say that this book covers almost all the concepts, and you can always come back and refer to it when you get doubts regarding the basics.</p>

</section>

</body>
```

```
</html>
```

As you can see, the two sections have got the same theme - HTML, but are very different in what they are trying to say.

Aside

Oftentimes you may have seen the main content being displayed in the centre or towards the left, with some minor related content being displayed in the sidebar. This is done with the help of the <aside> tag. This tag is used to display small sections of information that is related to the main topic, and can be placed at the sides.

```
<!DOCTYPE html>

<html>

<body>

<p>This is the main topic, about HTML.</p>

<aside>

 <h4>HTML</h4>

 <p>HTML is Hyper Text Markup Language</p>

</aside>

</body>
```

```
</html>
```

Details and Summary

This is the small arrow mark you might have seen, which when clicked, expands a small text box and displays additional information. Details is therefore, a way of adding information which the user can choose to see. The summary tag lets you add the title for the details tag. The best way to understand this is with an example:

```
<!DOCTYPE html>

<html>

<body>

<details>

  <summary>Click here for more info</summary>

  <p>This is the extra information.</p>

</details>

</body>

</html>
```

When you try this code, you will notice that the text in the summary gets displayed as the title, with the other text going into the expandable text box. This is how the details and summary works.

Figure and Figcaption

This is as easy as it gets. You can add an image, and attach a caption to it with the help of the figure and fig caption tags.

<!DOCTYPE html>

<html>

<body>

<p>This is your description. Instead of giving a caption for the image you are uploading as a description, it might be a better idea to use the <figcaption> tag as shown below.</p>

<figure>

  <img src="image.jpeg" alt="Enter Image" width="300" height="220">

  <figcaption>Image1: This is your caption.</figcaption>

</figure>

</body>

</html>

Conclusion

Creating a webpage is something that has been wreathed in mysticism and cyber mumbo jumbo for years, but I hope that I've shown you that it's not as scary as you might think. In fact, HTML is actually fairly straight forward. IF you're looking for a hobby that can really accomplish something and is easy to explain, then you've come to the right place. These are the foundations upon which you can build your webpage and push on to greater things like CSS, Java, JavaScript, C++, and the list goes on and on. Remember, that you can never really get in over your head if you master and truly understand what it is that you're working on in the moment.

If something doesn't make sense to you or is confusing, my best suggestion to you is to open up your TextEdit or Notepad and start working on it. Pull it up in your browser and have a look at what it does for your page. Taking everything step by step will inevitably lead you to the path of success. There is never a reason to jump ahead without fully understanding what it is that you've done.

If you ever find yourself having a need to get back to the basics or you just don't remember how to do something simple, come back to this book and have a look at the fundamentals. With everything that I have presented to you in this book, you should be able to get the grasp on the beginnings of a webpage and if you can get the beginning, it's just a matter of taking the next step piece by piece. So good luck and get out there and make an amazing webpage.

Thank you for Reading! I Need Your Help...

Dear Reader,

I Hope you Enjoyed **"HTML: Quick Start Guide Creating an Effective Website"**. I have to tell you, as an Author, I love feedback! I am always seeking ways to improve my current books and make the next ones better. It's readers like you who have the biggest impact on a book's success and development! So, tell me what you liked, what you loved, and even what you hated. I would love to hear from you, and I would like to ask you a favor, if you are so inclined, would you please share a minute to review my book. Loved it, Hated it - I'd just enjoy your feedback. As you May have gleaned from my books, reviews can be tough to come by these days and You the reader have the power make or break the success of a book. If you'd be so kind to CLICK HERE to review the book, I would greatly appreciate it! Thank you so much again for reading **"HTML: Quick Start Guide Creating an Effective Website"** and for spending time with me! I will see you in the next one!

Check Out More From The Publisher...

Social Media: Master Social Media Marketing - Facebook, Twitter, YouTube & Instagram

by Grant Kennedy

http://www.amazon.com/Social-Media-Marketing-Facebook-Instagram-ebook/dp/B018Y68SWS

Survival: The Survival Guide for Preppers, Make Yourself Ready Through Hunting, Fishing, Canning, and Foraging

by Jack Campbell

http://www.amazon.com/Survival-Preppers-Permaculture-Bushcraft-Hydroponics-ebook/dp/B01573FBP8

Krav Maga: Dominating Solutions to Real World Violence

by George Silva

http://www.amazon.com/Krav-Maga-Dominating-Solutions-Violence-ebook/dp/B01A2BL6CW

Day Trading: Dominate The Market - Stocks, Options, & Forex *by Warrick Liversedge*

http://www.amazon.com/Day-Trading-Dominate-Options-Covered-ebook/dp/B01A3LJCMM

SEO: Marketing Strategies to Dominate the First Page

by Grant Kennedy

http://www.amazon.com/SEO-Marketing-Strategies-analytics-optimization-ebook/dp/B01ACB7LQM